Our Everlasting Hope

Rev. Cleo Santiago, BCCC, BCPC

Discovering Hope
Despite Life's Tragedies

Table of Contents

Copyright © 2022 Rev. Cleo Santiago
Paperback ISBN: **978-1-7374637-7-1**
Ebook ISBN: **978-1-7374637-8-8**

Forward

An article I recently read supplied the following statistic: "Every year, roughly 14.8 million Americans experience depressive symptoms. These depressive symptoms can be mild, moderate, or severe. Among those who experience severe depressive symptoms, nearly 90% report some or serious difficulty with work, home, or social activities". These symptoms are often the result of people becoming discouraged with the current state of their lives. They believed they would be married with children or further in their careers. They expected to have finished school. They became discouraged when their reality did not meet their expectations.

"To be discouraged" means to lose confidence or enthusiasm and to become disheartened. Often, this occurs when someone is feeling overwhelmed by situations, circumstances, or life in general. Another destructive pattern that may lead to discouragement is our human tendency to allow our minds to become consumed by every adverse situation we may face. Other destructive patterns include an inability to stop thinking about past failures and disappointments. These "weights" hinder us from moving forward in life. Living in a state of constant discouragement can lead to feelings of hopelessness.

The journey out of discouragement begins when someone decides to come out of that state of mind and move forward. Every successful journey in life begins with hope.

We cannot afford to lose hope. Hopelessness leads to the loss of the will to live. This is why having hope in God is so important. Hope is God's lifeline to pull us out of discouragement and distress. "Our Everlasting Hope" is the perfect book for anyone that believes they need God's lifeline. In this book, you will learn how critical it is to have hope; not hope in yourself, your friends, or in this world, but hope in God. This book will teach you that God is the Only One that can give you "EVERLASTING HOPE" because hope is an everlasting promise from God.

Pastor Gavin Taylor
Lead Pastor of
The Love of Jesus Family Church
North Newark, NJ

INTRODUCTION:
Life of Tragedy, Life of Hope

A beautiful, athletic, seventeen-year-old student dove into the Chesapeake Bay on a warm summer day in 1967, which would change her life forever.

Misjudging the depth of the refreshing water, she hit her head on the rocky bottom and suffered a catastrophic injury. She broke her neck, severing her spinal cord, rendering her a person with paraplegia for life.

All the plans she made for her life were interrupted instantly. Dreams of college, a career, athletic pursuits, travel, marriage, and children were immediately crushed. Her world revolved not around the promising prospects of a girl on the brink of adulthood but hospitals and therapists, beds, wheelchairs, misery, and pain.

Two long years of rehabilitation followed. She endured surgery, traction, therapy, and painful processes designed to stabilize her broken body, prohibit further injury, and educate her to live without using her arms and legs.

For months she languished in sterile facilities as she came to terms with the extent of her injury:

- She would never walk.
- Never brush her teeth.
- Never feed herself, let alone cook a meal.
- She would have to rely on others to meet her most basic physical needs.
- An independent young woman wholly and suddenly dependent.

Depression set in, and how could it not? Her life as she knew it was over. The new life she faced from the perspective of her wheelchair looked miserable, lonely, and hopeless. Death began to look preferable, even attractive. Maybe an infection would take hold and end her suffering. Perhaps her diminished lung capacity would continue to decline until she could no longer breathe. Perhaps she would end it all herself.

But suicide wasn't even possible without using her arms and legs. She began ramming the electric wheelchair, to which she was bound, into walls with sheer anger and grief. Nothing would comfort her. There was no consolation.

Medicine offered no hope. Her spine could never be repaired, and her motor functions would never be restored. All the doctors, therapists, and treatments in the world could only, at their best, keep her comfortable, and even that was often a stretch.

Physical healing didn't come. What came was arguably a more astounding miracle than if Margaret had stood up from that wheelchair and began to walk.

She began to hope and pray for a miracle. Believing in God and having a vague notion of His omnipotence, she knew it was possible. Crying out to Him day and night, she begged him to heal her broken body and end her suffering, one way or another.

God heard the prayers of Margaret Davis over fifty years ago. He met her in her wheelchair and answered her cries for help. Oh, how she prayed!

What came was hope.

Hope amid tremendous suffering. Hope despite an uncertain future. Hope in the middle of tragedy. Hope regardless of the pain, fear, doubt, misery, disappointment, and grief.

Her hope was not in modern medicine or miraculous healing. Her hope in the God who encountered her in that wheelchair, comforted her during her pain and despair, and gave her a future worth living.

- She began to paint with a brush clenched between her teeth.
- She began to write her story.
- She began to study the Word of God with a voracious appetite for His truth.
- She began to think outside of herself and care for others with disabilities.
- Books, ministries, and speaking engagements followed.

She became an inspiration.

In Margaret's book, "Hope...The Best of Things," she writes, "Oh, how we need to grasp the soul-edifying hope found in the Scriptures-- not only grasp it but allow the hope of God's Word to fill and overflow our hearts, transforming us into people who are confident and at peace with themselves, their God, and their circumstances."

What is this "soul-edifying hope" that she writes about and lives out to this day? How can her soul be enlightened and have hope after living for more than fifty years immobilized in a wheelchair?

Margaret found it in the pages of God's Word. It changed her life and the lives of countless others which her ministry has touched.

Let's dig into His Word and see what it says about this little four-letter word: **Hope**.

Reflection

Introduction

What comes to mind when you hear the word "hope?"

How would you define hope in your own words?

On a scale of 1-10, 1 being the least hopeful and 10 being the most hopeful, how hopeful of a person are you and give examples for the number you have chosen?

How do you think you would cope with a tragedy like the one that paralyzed Margaret Davis?

Describe a situation in your life where you felt utterly hopeless? How did you cope with it?

What do you hope to glean from this study?

Chapter 1
Hope-Beyond the Platitudes

Verse for Today

'I have set the Lord always before me: because he is at my right hand, I shall not be moved. Therefore, my heart is glad, and my glory rejoiceth: my flesh also shall rest in hope."

Psalm 16:8-9

Reflection

We throw the word "hope" around all the time.

We use it in trite little phrases offering well wishes to others and expressing our desire for positive outcomes:

- "We hope the ball game doesn't get rained out."
- "I hope the results of your biopsy is negative."
- "The kids hope they are getting a puppy for Christmas."
- "We are hoping for the best."
- "I hope you have a nice day!"

Then there are the platitudes about hope. You'll find them on greeting cards, plaques to hang on the office wall, and inspirational calendars offering words of encouragement.

- "Once you choose hope anything's possible". – Christopher Reeve
- Hope is the last thing ever lost." - Italian proverb
- "When the world says, "Give up," Hope whispers, "Try it one more time." – Author Unknown
- Hope is being able to see that there is light despite all the darkness." – Desmond Tutu

But do any of these things describe the "soul-edifying hope" that Margaret Davis found while newly bound to a wheelchair?

Is this the hope that could change the course of a tragically altered life, causing a woman to survive and thrive?

The hope that Margaret found is the same hope that David speaks of in Psalm 16, where he declares, *"my flesh also rests in hope."* While not paralyzed, he was stricken in many ways and suffered terrible hardships, some of his own making. Yet he found rest in that soul-edifying hope.

This is not the word hope used in the common language of well wishes and desires. This is the hope found only in the Lord.

It is the life-changing, soul-edifying, rest-inducing hope found only in God.

Prayer

The God of all hope, I confess. I misuse this little word all the time. Saying that I hope for trite desires like good weather, gifts, and good times is a misuse of this powerful word.

I confess that I often put my hope in all the wrong things. I put my hope in an easy life, problems disappearing, and things going my way.

Hoping in the things of this world is a practice in futility. This world is evil, broken, fading, and dying. If my hope is bound up in the things of this world, like money, medicine, people, and things, I know, I will continue to be sorely disappointed.

You offer a more profound, more faithful, greater hope. The hope that has changed people's lives like Margaret Davis is far greater than anything this world offers. Such hope makes sense only in the light of Your Word, character, and work.

Please help me to understand this hope as I study it here. I want to live a life marked by it. I want it to change me. I want it to transform my daily life.

I want to share it with others. Please help me cling to your hope, for in it, my soul will rest, and my flesh will be at ease. In the name of Jesus, who is my hope, I pray. Amen.

Reflection
Chapter 1 Hope Beyond the Platitudes

How does the word "hope" used in everyday language compare with the "hope" found in the Scriptures?

Look at Psalm 16:8-9. Describe the five actions that David takes which lead to hope.

How can you put some of these practices into action in your own life?

CHAPTER 2
Biblical Hope Defined

Verse for Today

"This I recall to my mind, therefore have I hope. It is of the Lord's mercies that we are not consumed, because his compassions fail not. They are new every morning: great is thy faithfulness. The Lord is my portion, saith my soul; therefore, will I hope in him."

Lamentations 3 :21-24

Reflection

When we use the word "hope" in our daily lives, it usually implies a level of uncertainty:

- Hoping for good weather means that the weather report casts doubt, and the clouds gather in the distance.
- Hoping for a favorable prognosis at the doctor's office means the results are pending and could go either way.
- Hoping for that large bonus at work means the boss is still crunching the numbers at the year's end, and the final budget is in doubt.

When we say we are hoping, it implies doubting because we are!

Hope with such uncertainty is not the hope found in the Scriptures. It is not the hope that transformed the life of Margaret, birthing fifty-plus years of fruitful ministry which has given hope to countless others suffering similar disabilities and hardships.

Biblical hope is more than just crossing our fingers, closing our eyes, and wishing for the best, because it is a hope rooted in the person and character of God. Biblical hope has confidence, not doubt, because of who God is and what God has said.

God has so many names which all reflect his character:

- God is love.
- He is our provider.
- He is our protector.
- He is our friend.
- God is all-powerful, all-knowing,
  And all present.
- God is our Father, Savior, healer,
  And deliverer.

God is all these things and so much more. When we believe in Him and all that He is, putting our trust in Him, we find hope which goes far beyond wishful thinking. It will change our lives.

The writer of Lamentations finds hope during destruction, loss, misery, and grief. How?

By remembering all that God has done:

- He remembers the mercy of God, new every single morning.
- He remembers the compassion of God, which never fails.
- He remembers the faithfulness of God, so great in every circumstance.

We can do the same and find confident hope in the Lord, which will transform our lives.

Prayer

Heavenly Father, the hope the world has to offer is always clouded by doubt. I cannot have confidence in it, and it will always let me down. But you are different.

God, I know I can have confidence in you when I root that hope in your character. You are good, merciful, loving, gracious, compassionate, just, and sovereign. You are many more things, good things that allow me to hope in you confidently.

Fear causes me distress. Please help me to remember all that you are and all that you have done. Remind me of your new mercies every morning, your compassion that never fails, and your faithfulness in all circumstances so I can confidently hope in you.

Help me fight the urge to put my hope in temporal things that will fail me. People, money, and everything in this world are not worthy of my hope in You because they will always disappoint me. They are flawed. You are my one true hope.

Heavenly Father, be the God who consoles me today. Help me learn more about who you are, what you have said, and what you have done so that my certainty in you will not waiver. Bring back to my remembrance these things as I put my hope in you today.

I pray in the name of my great God and Savior, Jesus Christ. Amen.

Reflection
Chapter 2 Biblical Hope Defined

Look up the following Scriptures. Write down what each Scripture teaches us about God's character.

Genesis 22:9-14

1 John 4:7-10

Psalm 119:65-68

Judges 6:16-24

Look up the following Scriptures. Write down what each Scripture teaches us about God's character.

Revelation 4:8-11

Exodus 15:22-26

Deuteronomy 4:29-31

Ephesians 1:5-8

Look up the following Scriptures. Write down what each Scripture teaches us about God's character.

2 Corinthians 1:3-4

How does reading these attributes of God help you have hope?

CHAPTER 3:
A Long-Suffering Hope

Verse for Today

"(Abraham) Who against hope believed in hope, that he might become the father of many nations, according to that which was spoken, So shall thy seed be."

Romans 4:18

Reflection

The Genesis account of the life of Abraham teaches us much about hope. God called Abraham the father of many nations and a blessing to all the people of the earth. Abraham believed in God, and Genesis 15:6 tells us **"...he counted it to him for righteousness."**

Abraham and his wife Sarah were elderly, far beyond their childbearing years. Stricken and infertile. They had no children and believed they never would.

Until God gave them hope.
God promised Abraham and Sarah an heir, and they clung to that hope. Yet the years came and went without a baby.

Gazing at the countless stars in the sky, God showed Abraham the vast number of his offspring that would walk the face of the earth. It was remarkable, unfathomable, and hopeful. But more childless years followed.

They followed God faithfully to Egypt and back, leading their family and clinging to God's promise. Still, no baby.

Taking matters into their own hands, Abraham fathered a child by Hagar. This moment of hopelessness and faithlessness displeased the Lord, for this was not the promised son nor how he would come. Abraham would have to wait longer still.

He clung to hope, which increased his faith. Faith and hope go hand in hand in the scriptures.

Hebrews 11:1 teaches us, **"Now faith is the substance of things hoped for, the evidence of things not seen."** Faith gave substance to Abraham's hope, strengthening it for more waiting.

We have hope because we have faith.
Likewise, we have faith because we hope.
Faith in the one true God breeds hope.

Paul tells us in Romans chapter four that
Abraham's hope was against all hope. He was
hoping in a hopeless situation. As the years
ticked by, they lost hope, and their aging
bodies continued to fail. Any outsider looking
into the life of this elderly, infertile couple would
say that there was absolutely no hope that they
could produce a child!

But this wasn't a false hope or a pipe dream.
This confident hope was rooted in the promise
and character of the God that Abraham knew
intimately. Abraham's faith in God produced a
long-suffering hope; we are his heirs because
of it!

Prayer

God of Abraham, Isaac, and Jacob, the story of these forefathers gives me greater faith and hope in you. You promised Abraham a son, and you always keep your promises. Thank you for your plan of redemption and the part this story plays in it.

Abraham believed you but was not perfect. His faith wavered as he waited for you to fulfill your promise, which is such an encouragement to me!

My faith wavers all the time when I take my eyes off you. Forgive me for looking to other hopes that will fail me rather than keeping my eyes and heart fixed on you. You will never forget me.

Please help me not to lose hope and take matters into my own hands. There are things I have waited for, for so long. There are unfulfilled longings, broken dreams, and deferred plans. Please strengthen my hope and encourage my faith.

Remind me of your love, faithfulness, mercy, and grace. I can hope for you because I have tasted and seen that you are good. Please remind me of this goodness when my hope starts to fail me.

You are the God of all hope, and I trust you. This is not a false hope or a pipe dream, but a confident hope in who you are and what you have done.

My faith is in you, and therefore I have hope. May it be so all the days of my life that I pray in the name of Jesus Christ. Amen.

Reflection
Chapter 3: A Long-Suffering Hope

Read Romans 4:18-25. Reflect upon the statement "Against all hope, Abraham in hope believed..." Is this a contradiction? Why or why not?

Read Genesis 16:1-4 and Genesis 17:15-19. God promised Abram and Sarai a son, but they took matters into their own hands when it did not happen at a time they felt it should have taken place. How do you explain this apparent loss of faith?

Read Hebrews 11:1.
Explain this definition of faith in your own
words.

Explain how faith and hope go hand in hand.

Read 1 Corinthians 13, the famous chapter on love.

Why is love greater than faith and hope?

How do faith, hope, and love interact in your life?

CHAPTER 4
Hope In God's Word

Verse for Today

"For whatsoever things were written aforetime were written for our learning, that we through patience and comfort of the scriptures might have hope."

Romans 15:4

Reflection

Laying in her bed in a rehab facility months after the catastrophic accident left her paralyzed, Margaret Davis began to find hope.

This newly awakened hope was not found in a medical miracle or promising therapy. It began in the same Scriptures she had heard in church all her life. Friends and family began to share with her the promises of God established in the Scripture, which quickened the hope she had been missing within her.

The Apostle Paul tells us of the hope found in the Scriptures in Romans 15:4. This verse gives us a three-part understanding of how the Scriptures lead us to have hope.

He first tells us that the Scriptures were written for our learning.

- We are confident from other passages, like in Paul's second letter to Timothy, which says, *"All Scripture is given by inspiration of God, and is profitable for doctrine, for reproof, for correction, for instruction in righteousness:*

  That the man of God may be perfect, thoroughly furnished unto all good works." (2 Timothy 3:16-17)

- We have the whole counsel of God's Word to instruct us in countless ways. Through it, we learn about God's character and purpose for creation. We know of His great plan of redemption through Jesus. We learn history, poetry, and doctrine.

- We are corrected, instructed, and changed when we take it to heart and live by it.

Paul then speaks about the patience we can find through the scriptures.

- Other versions of the Bible use the word endurance rather than patience. We can endure in this life when we remember what God has done for us, described throughout the Scriptures' pages. We can also endure as we look ahead to the promised life when we put our faith in Jesus.

- Patience and endurance flow from a deep and abiding head and heart knowledge that comes from knowing God's Word.

- Finally, Paul tells us that the Word can bring us comfort. Countless passages speak of God's great love for His people, His grace poured out on them, and His mercy shown to them. These promises abound throughout the Scriptures, which God always keeps, and we can cling to.

- His Word is true, beautiful, comforting, reassuring, and full of hope.

- Learning the Scriptures encourages us to endure through this life and find comfort in God, which ultimately leads to hope.

Therefore, the Psalmist can sing, *"I wait for the LORD, my whole being waits, and in His word, I put my hope."* (Psalm 130:5)

Prayer

Heavenly Father, you have seen fit to give us your holy and abiding Word. You did not need to do this, yet out of your great love for us, you have revealed yourself through the Scriptures. Thank you for the Scriptures. Please renew my desire for your Word.

Your Word is for my direction, and I have much to gain from it. I confess that I have not loved your Word as I should. I have not handled it carefully, nor have I cherished it. I must learn much from it, so I ask you to teach me. Surround me with individuals to help me understand and learn from the Scriptures.

I can endure through this life with the help of your Word. Throughout the Scriptures, I find your love for me, your plan of redemption, and your desire for me to abide in you. These truths and many more make me want to know you more deeply.

I am comforted by your Spirit. Your love, grace, mercy, faithfulness, goodness, and power bring me comfort that I cannot find in this world. You are my peace and comfort amid this stormy life.

I become increasingly hopeful by learning your Word, enduring it, and finding solace in it! Clinging to your Word leads me to hope in you, and I rejoice.

Please teach me more as I embrace your Word and grow in my hope. In the name of Jesus, my hope, I pray. Amen.

Reflection
Chapter 4: Hope in God's Word

Look up the following Scriptures. Write what they teach us about God's Word.

Hebrews 4:12

Psalm 119:105

James 1:22-25

Isaiah 40:6-8

Look up the following Scriptures. Write what they teach us about God's Word.

Psalm 18:30

Matthew 4:4

Matthew 7:24-29

Psalm 19:7

How does reading these Scriptures help you have hope in God's word?

CHAPTER 5
Hope in the Hardships

Verse for Today

"...but we glory in tribulations also: knowing that tribulation worketh patience; And patience, experience; and experience, hope: And hope maketh not ashamed; because the love of God is shed abroad in our hearts by the Holy Ghost which is given unto us."

Romans 5:3-5

Reflection

Holding onto hope in great suffering is one of life's most complicated challenges. We like to throw all those platitudes around when someone is facing a tragedy or trial. We mean to encourage and love, but statements like "don't lose hope" or "hold onto hope" often sound empty and hollow to someone in a pit of despair.

Biblical hope held out to a suffering person is anything but empty or hollow.

The hope of life in Christ is the only real hope we must cling to here on earth when things like medicine, money, and people fail us left and right.

The Apostle Paul again informs us about hope in chapter five of his letter to the Romans. He goes so far as to say we can rejoice in our trials because they will lead us to hope. Rejoice in trials and tribulations. How can this be?

It sounds complete and utter nonsense to speak of rejoicing when we face troubles. No one rejoices when the doctor diagnoses cancer. No one rejoices as they sign the bankruptcy papers. No one rejoices when a beloved spouse walks away, or a tornado hits the house.

Would Margaret rejoice as she faced decades in a wheelchair, unable even to brush her teeth? She would, and she does.

She says "NO"! My request for miraculous physical healing has meant purged transgression, a love for the lost, increased compassion, stretched hope, an appetite for grace, an increase of faith, a joyful longing for heaven, a desire to serve, a delight in prayer, and a hunger for his Word. Oh, bless the stern schoolmaster that is my wheelchair! It's all to the praise, the more profound healing in Christ."

Margaret found that God was doing more significant work in her life than miraculous healing, and she could rejoice in it just as Paul instructs in the book of Romans.

Suffering produces endurance, that long-suffering patience we've already discussed. The only way to get past a trial is to keep walking through it. Just like with physical exercise, the more you walk, the more you can walk. Your endurance grows to where you can walk miles without breaking a sweat. So, it is with suffering.

That endurance then produces experience and develops character. As we walk through a trial clinging to God and learning from His Word, we are strengthened in the faith and made to be more like Jesus. He endured the ultimate suffering, and we become more like him as we suffer. God is at work!

Character produces a hope that does not put us to shame. Remember, this is not a false hope or a pipe dream. That kind of hope can certainly put us to shame as we fall flat on our faces in utter disappointment.

But the hope found in God never puts us to shame because, at the end of it, we find Him and His great love for us.

Prayer

God of all hope, you are at work in me amidst my trials. I confess that this is hard for me to remember when life is so hard. All I see is the pain and anguish, and I want relief. Help me to remember that this trial is for my good and your glory.

You are sanctifying me through my suffering, making me more like Jesus. He endured the ultimate suffering on the cross for my sins, and I know my trials pale compared to that grief and pain. Jesus was separated from you on the cross, suffering I will never have to endure because of Him. Thank you for that!

This suffering is producing endurance in me. Help me patiently suffer, knowing that you are stretching, growing, and making me the person you want me to be.

Endurance through this trial is producing character in me. You are growing me to be more like Jesus.

You are cleansing me daily. You are compelling me to deny the old self and live for you. You are sanctifying me. I have hope in spite of my suffering because you are at work in me, and I rejoice.

This trial is thorny. This suffering is long. This pain is real. Yet I delight in the midst of it because you are at work in my heart.

Please help me not fight against this work of grace. Instead, allow me to seek and find you as you walk through it with me. In Jesus' name, I pray. Amen.

Reflection
Chapter 5: Hope in the Hardships

Read Romans 5:1-9. Use it to answer the following questions.

How have you been justified?

How do you have peace?

How have you gained access to grace?

What are you to boast in?

What are you to glory in?

What does suffering produce?

What does perseverance produce?

What does character produce?

Why does hope not put us to shame?

How did God demonstrate His love for you?

How have you been reconciled to God?

Meditate upon these remarkable truths. How does this give you hope in your trials?

CHAPTER 6
A Future Hope

Verse for Today

"Blessed be the God and Father of our Lord Jesus Christ, which according to his abundant mercy hath begotten us again unto a lively hope by the resurrection of Jesus Christ from the dead, To an inheritance incorruptible, and undefiled, and that fadeth not away, reserved in heaven for you."

1 Peter 1:3-4

Reflection

God's abundant mercy has birthed us into a living hope. Peter begins his first letter with this incredible truth. This Biblical hope is alive because Jesus himself is alive!

Peter could speak of this hope perhaps better than anyone. This humble fisherman was an eyewitness to the most remarkable displays of God's power. He stood beside the tomb as Lazarus emerged. He rejoiced as Jairus received his daughter back into his arms. He witnessed healings, deliverances, and transformations at the hand of Jesus.

Peter met the resurrected Jesus, who received him into His arms despite his denial. His life had been transformed by the life, death, and resurrection of his master, and the hope he found in Jesus would lead him to his cross years later.

This living hope that Peter spoke of is rooted in the person and work of Jesus. Hope in the things of this world will fade, die, and disappoint, but not this Jesus' hope.

It is an everlasting hope that will not fade or fail. Peter tells us that it is incorruptible and undefiled. It is perfect in every way because Jesus is perfect in every way. It is kept in heaven for us and awaits those of us who have put our faith in Jesus.

Sometimes we get a little peek of our future hope here on earth. The joys and blessings we experience here are a little taste of what's to come. The good gifts God gives us here are a pale shadow of the glory that awaits us in heaven.

Margaret says, "The best we can hope for in this life is a knothole glimpse at the shining realities ahead. Yet a glance is enough. It's enough to convince our hearts that whatever sufferings and sorrow currently assail us aren't worthy of comparison to that which waits over the horizon."

We find our living hope in Jesus, who endured the ultimate suffering on our behalf. Those who believe in Him can hope confidently that an inheritance awaits when in heaven. This hope helps us to stay in whatever trials we face here on earth as we look to Jesus.

The little glimpses of heaven we see here on earth are a taste of what's to come.

Prayer

Father God, according to your great mercy, you have caused me to be born again into a living hope. I now have everlasting hope in you through the work of your Son, Jesus, on the cross. I don't deserve this, but I thank you for it.

An inheritance awaits me in heaven because I have put my faith in you. I fall short of your glory all the time.

I am undeserving of your grace and love, yet you lavish it upon me all the time and I rejoice that you have seen fit to make me your child and your inheritor.

The things in this world cannot corrupt the inheritance you keep in heaven for me. It is not based on my goodness, righteousness, or works. It is based on Jesus 'goodness, His righteousness, and His work on the cross on my behalf. Thank you for Jesus, your perfect son who died for my imperfections.

Please help me not put my hope in the little glimpses of heaven I see here on earth. You have given me good gifts, even amid my troubles. Yet even the best of these gifts' pale in comparison to what you hold for me in heaven. Please give me a longing for the eternal joy found only at your right hand.

I rejoice in you and your generous, splendid love and grace. Because you have loved me and are at work in my heart.

I can have confident hope in you, and my future is in your hands. Thank you for this living hope. Help me to abide in it, in the name of Jesus, my hope, I pray. Amen.

Reflection
Chapter 6: A Future Hope

What image do you have of heaven? Has it been informed by the Bible or by our culture?

Do you fear death? Why or why not?

Read 1 Peter 1:3-4. Describe in your own words the inheritance that believers in Christ are due to receive.

Are there things in your life that give you glimpses of heaven? What are they and how will heaven be different?

Read Revelation 21:1-7.

How does this image of heaven give you hope?

CONCLUSION
Steadfast in Hope

The steadfast hope found in God is impossible for people to understand unless they have experienced His love, grace, and mercy firsthand for themselves.

Apart from God, our only hope can be found in the things of this world, which will always let us down.

- When medicine is no longer useful.
- Economies collapse.
- People die.
- Relationships crumble.
- Natural disasters occur.

We live in a fallen world, and any hope it offers is finite and fallible.

The hope found in God described in His Word is everlasting because He is eternal.

It is good because He is good.

It can be depended upon because He never fails us.

When we put our faith in Jesus Christ, we can dwell in the hope of His love, grace, and mercy despite our tragedies.

Paul says in Romans 15:13, *"Now the God of hope fill you with all joy and peace in believing, that ye may abound in hope, through the power of the Holy Ghost."*

The joy and peace of God come with believing in Him through the power of the Holy Spirit, and we abound in everlasting hope.

~ Rev. Cleo Santiago, BCCC, BCPC

To the God of Hope, be the praise and glory forever.

Endorsement

It would be great if whatever we have not dealt with by midnight would just "POOF" and disappear before morning. Unfortunately, that's not how life works. Sometimes it seems like yesterday's problems, issues, difficulties, and challenges are staring us down as soon as we open our eyes each day – stalking us – waiting to see what we are going to do about them, how we are going to address and resolve each one and when.

Some persons can endure the pressure, even while fear and uncertainty loom about, seeking to confuse. Others, consumed by it all, sadly choose to end it all rather than wait another day. It also seems that "every time we turn around," another precious person's life has ended by their own hand. The living cannot presume to know why. The specifics of the reasoning that led to such a decision will remain a mystery forever.

Like most, my family had our struggles, but that never stopped my parents from reminding me constantly to find ways to leave the world better than how I found it. Rev. Cleo Santiago, BCCC, BCPC, also know this well. Hope sustains him as the primary caregiver of his beloved mother, who was severely injured in a car accident in 2001, suffering an injury to 15% of her brain. Rev. Cleo Santiago and I met through service projects worked on by our respective families. Having served disadvantaged communities for years, Rev. Santiago and I have seen people at their best and worst. An absence of hope is, more often than not, the root cause of the latter.

As much as this present work by Rev. Cleo Santiago is about the need for "hope," the unfortunate prevalence of "hopelessness" cannot be ignored. It is an undeniable fact: Hope. We cannot live without it. How does one get over grief? How does one overcome depression? How does one reclaim hope amid debilitating sickness, loss, or tragedy? In a world that sees no future, this book will remind you that you do have a lot. In a world full of darkness, this book reminds us that God is with us; His Hand will guide us. This book encourages us to look to Jesus, Our Everlasting Hope.

Abraham Abe' Lopez,

President of the Florida Debate Initiative, a not-for-profit organization, working to provide students with opportunities to take part in competitive debate and public speaking.

About The Author

The Rev. Cleo J. Santiago, BCCC, BCPC

The Rev. Cleo Santiago is a Board-Certified Clinical Chaplain and Pastoral Counselor who works in Hospice care & with the Department of Corrections. Rev. Santiago provides Pastoral care counseling, helping those under his care find meaning in their experiences. Fluent in Spanish and English, he can communicate and engage with persons across cultural boundaries.

For five years, The Rev. Santiago served in the local Church pastorate ministry of a non-denominational church in the Town of Bayonne. He is an active community member specializing in urban ministries and addictions. His love for the community led him to become the Chairperson for Community Outreach for the Latino Ministers of New Jersey for Justice. He is also a Board Delegate for New Jersey Center for Empowerment and Community Development. The Rev. Santiago is the Convener for the New Jersey Chapter of the Visiting Chaplains' Association.

As an ordained minister who has transitioned to the Lutheran Orthodox Church NY-NJ, the Rev. Santiago has completed his Clinical Training at Hackensack Meridian Health Palisades Medical Center with the College of Pastoral Supervision and Psychotherapy. The Rev. Santiago continues to provide pastoral and bereavement counseling at Hackensack Meridian Health Palisades Medical Center.

The Rev. Santiago was born in New Jersey, raised in Puerto Rico, and has been active in empowering urban communities since 2004. He continues to partner with local community leaders and ministries to help community members heal from loss, pain, and addiction. He has integrated his life experience with his Clinical Training in the care and counseling of the community. The Rev. Cleo Santiago is married to Lizzette Santiago with three children.

www.ingramcontent.com/pod-product-compliance
Lightning Source LLC
Chambersburg PA
CBHW071107090426
42737CB00013B/2519